Cinder & Ivy

Poetry and Prose for the beautifully Broken

Phaedra Michaud

TABLE OF CONTENTS

Dedication

To my father,

For your unwavering love, your quiet strength, and the endless wisdom you've shared.

You taught me what it means to stand tall in the face of life's storms, to endure with grace, and to discover beauty even in brokenness.

You have been a steady presence, a constant voice guiding me through life's uncertainties— reminding me that I am capable and enough, even when the world feels heavy.

I am forever your hummingbird girl, flitting through life with the lessons you've woven into my soul: how to savor sweetness in fleeting moments, how it's okay to be vulnerable yet fierce, and how to always return to the places that matter most.

Thank you for choosing me to be your daughter, and for showing me that love—even in its imperfections—is the most unshakable bond we share.

And to all the children—past, present, and future—who are in foster care, navigating broken adoptions, or lost in the empty shadows of this world:

I see you, because I was you.

Know that you are more than your circumstances, and that your dreams are worth pursuing.

This book is for you—a testament that hope and resilience can transform even the darkest nights.

Prologue

I began as a cinder—a smoldering remnant of what life was meant to be.

A ward of the state, I was passed from place to place, a fragile ember caught in winds too harsh to hold me. The abuse, the neglect, the cold indifference—they were the flames that burned away the innocence of my childhood, leaving only ash. The words meant to wound, the hands that hurt, the promises that always broke—they settled in my soul like cinders, smoldering quietly, refusing to die.

And yet, from the ashes, something began to grow: ivy—delicate, fierce, unyielding. It crept through the cracks of my pain, climbing toward a light I couldn't see but somehow knew was there. It whispered resilience into the quiet, wove beauty through the brokenness, and anchored me when the weight of it all threatened to pull me under.

The world saw only the cinders—fragments of a life burned down to nothing. Yet in the ruins, I began to write. Words scribbled on scraps of paper became my rebellion, my sanctuary, my proof that something within me still lived. The abuse was the fire, but the words were the ivy—wrapping around my heart, refusing to let go. They became my bloom, my defiance, my answer to a world that tried to silence me.

And now, here I stand—no longer just a cinder, no longer merely the remains of what was lost.

I am the ivy that grew despite the flames. I am the voice that rose from the ashes, the strength that sprouted where the world believed nothing could survive. These pages hold my story—of pain that shaped me, resilience that saved me, and haunting beauty that emerged from devastation.

This is for those who still feel like cinders, trapped in the fires of life's cruelty. This is for those still waiting to bloom, who cannot yet see the ivy climbing within them.

This is proof that even in the ashes, something beautiful can rise.

This is my story—and perhaps, in some way, it is yours too.

Monsters

No matter how far I come,

they linger in the crevices of my mind—

predators waiting to strike,

reviving the rush of traumas once endured.

They remind me constantly that I will never be whole.

Each hand that removed a piece of me,

each touch that burned away my innocence,

each strike that became the catalyst of my undoing—

all haunt me with the memory of a soul once complete,

before terror rained upon my skin

and tore my core from my chest.

I pretend to remember her.

Sometimes I even pretend to be her.

Smiles, rarely unforced.

Intimacy, my grand performance.

Love, my constant stage.

They never suspect.

My metaphoric Oscars,

stacked to oblivion in my mind.

And the monsters laugh,

knowing they control the show—

a puppet to pain, cloaked in a shroud of false self-love.

Oh, how they love to watch me dance in the flames they created.

Senses

I miss you.

Words so simple,

yet heavy with nostalgia that drapes the soul

in moments unavoidable.

A scent on the air,

dancing within its distracting aroma,

opening the heart to currents long buried

but ever burning—

embers smoldering amid the ashes of heartbreak.

Oh, how fickle a smell,

to bring you back to me so intrusively,

in a reel of pictures scattered

across translucent sheets,

playing intensely

through the corridors of my conscious mind.

The Wall

Loving you was never simple.

The walls you built from the remnants of broken
love past

were jagged shale against my already wounded
heart.

But climb I tried.

Like madness, I fell—consumed by your silent
intrigue,

your gaze that held a thousand words,

all calling to my soul to hear them.

I ascended your monstrosity of a wall,

leaving pieces of myself flayed away

by the arctic conditions of your so-called love.

With those torn fragments, I tried to mend you—

foolishly believing you might open

to the comforts of my sincerity.

Bits of my very own light

descended behind me,

and I gave no thought to what happens

when there is no more light,

no more pieces left to repair with.

No—loving you was never simple.

And I am still lost, fragmented,

fallen in the tremors of your bitterness.

I reach no more.

Entwined

Our paths crossed like two wandering spirits, lost
in the darkness;

yet the instant our gazes met, a sense of peace
washed over us.

We are one spirit, our hearts beating in harmony—

an unending love that was always destined to last.

You make me feel enough, no matter how hard life
gets

or how heavy the world becomes.

We move through agony with laughter and with
dance,

our love a radiant beacon, illuminating the path
through the storm.

Our flames dance, flash, and rise—

an eternal fire that endures through all things.

Together we stand, never to part,

two halves of one heart.

The love we share is a delicately woven tapestry:

a tender hug, a silent prayer,

every moment savored, every touch cherished.

The depth of our love surpasses understanding.

There is no love quite like ours—

we are twin flames, a mystery to the world,

but a truth we live with every breath.

Through every season, through every storm,

this is our story:

a love that thrives in all weather.

Nostalgia

Dreams get caught in the grooves of longing,

skipping time like a worn-out needle on old vinyl.

I find solace in the past,

where broken echoes and faded promises drift
away.

The needle presses down,

tracing fractures in a fragile existence.

The vinyl is torn and scarred,

a map of regrets etched in superficial wounds.

I walk through memory's corridors,

floorboards groaning beneath me—

their creaks a mournful dirge,

as shadows dance with spectral grace along the
walls.

Dreams appear fragile, brittle under dark
moonlight.

Each shard of porcelain on the forest floor

holds a thousand regrets.

Frozen moments linger like teardrops on a faded
photograph,

fluttering just out of reach—

fragile as butterflies evading desperate hands.

I chase their murmurs through wildflower
meadows,

barefoot, defenseless.

Petals, soft as secrets, cradle unseen pain

and release a fragrance that lingers in the soul.

As twilight deepens, the needle tires,

creating a slow waltz of longing and loss.

Dreams fade like whispered breaths,

leaving only a lingering ache.

Dreams—like a needle spinning its sorrowful
song—

weave haunting melodies that echo

through the hollow chambers of my being.

And as a captive, I find strange comfort

in the tears they carve into my soul.

In The Garden

Tattered remnants of a heart once full,

dreams staggered, beaten into submission

by the very love that keeps it pumping.

False expectations, dressed in pretty words at first,

intentions clouded by doubt cruelly inflicted.

Never able to measure up.

Never able to feel embraced.

Icicles form upon my cheeks

from the freeze of your callous words.

I stand in silent resilience

while you admire another's garden—

doting on it with encouragement,

patience, and smiles—

while the breath leaves my sails

a little more each time.

For if you think so little of me,

then I must be insignificant.

Because if I were relevant, surely

I would see your face light up

with delicious emotional currents—

instead of your eyes passing through me,

a glance of annoyed inconvenience.

I wish I were the rose garden,

not the weed you see me as.

How I have longed for you to close your eyes

and breathe me in

the way you do the fragrance of honeysuckle.

To touch me with perfect delicacy,

as you do when admiring daffodils,

their petals must entice you so.

And oh—to be looked at as you gaze upon the

rolling hills,

bathed in twilight.

I watch the light catch in your eyes,

sly and shimmering,

betrayed by winds that stir them to dance.

I understand, though.

The weed is dependent,

steadfast, always returning,

even in its intrusion.

The flowers—erratic in their beauty—

remain the ones you choose.

Oh, to be the rose.

Forest

In the shadowed embrace of the woods, I ran—

each footfall a frantic heartbeat.

The damp earth clung to my skin,

an urgent whisper of danger pressing close behind.

Branches clawed at me, sharp as daggers.

The predator prowled—its breath, a heavy fog.

Every rustle carried a sinister promise of pain.

I ducked beneath the gnarled arms of ancient trees,

my chest heaving,

moonlight casting silver wounds across the path.

Pressed against the bark, trembling,

I wondered—

was I only a flicker of light

in its insatiable night?

Memories of suffering surged like a tidal wave,

choking me,

anchoring my spirit in dread.

Each heartbeat became a desperate plea for
survival,

each pulse a reminder of my scars.

And yet—a flicker of defiance sparked within.

The shadows screamed with the agony of my past,

but still, I rose.

The woods became my sanctuary,
a battleground where pain forged strength.

A wild heart—fierce, unbroken, free.

In this world of shadows,

I reclaimed my light,

and let it blaze

with the full potency of my will.

Forever Pretty

Fresh grown must look pretty.

Must be clean, smell sweet—

only to be defiled

by tainted hands,

strangers with thirty pieces of silver.

A pristine flower,

budding, not yet bloomed.

Peeled, petal by petal,

until her energy is ravished

and only the twisted stem remains.

Stay pretty.

Stay obedient.

Escape means death of the body.

Remaining means death of the soul.

What's right or wrong when you already live in
hell?

Pain can be a comfort

when it comes with food for the week.

Stay pretty.

Stay entertaining.

Lose intrigue, get disposed of.

All kids fear rejection.

But not many fear

taking their last breath

because of it.

Stay pretty.

Stay desired.

Learn to seduce before you learn to read.

Learn to please them,

to survive—

and see home again.

Stay pretty.

Stay dreaming.

For being awake is the nightmare, where the

monsters are real. Dream hard,

keep your light.

Take heart—roots regrow.

You can bloom again.

Never the same,

but beautiful in your existence. You stayed pretty.

Blessed.

Mystery

A tremor quivered in my chest,

as I faced the haunting memories that lingered.

All the chaos inside me,

like a tempest raging, clawing at my spirit.

I thought I'd never find solace—oh, how naïve.

Buried beneath the delightful weight of despair,

every shadow whispered my deepest failures,

every echo mocked me as I gasped for breath.

How charming.

Yet from the shadows, a whisper crept,

like moonlight filtering through tangled trees—

a delicate promise dancing upon my skin.

My heart, once shattered and burdened,

now stirred, filled with mystery.

Embracing the jagged scars etched into my soul,

I found beauty in the darkness I bore—

a tapestry woven with threads of resilience,

a passionate love letter to the woman I now adore.

Truly poetic.

Did the darkness ever truly define me?

Or was it merely a fleeting shadow I wore?

Now I stand tall, a phoenix rising from ashes—

a woman reborn, fierce, and ready to soar.

What a plot twist!

For I know I deserve the profound peace I seek,

not just a flicker of light piercing the void.

So I'll gather the fragments of my spirit

and nurture a vibrant garden where my soul can

thrive.

How cliché—yet so true.

Invisibly Yours

Like dawn's merciless light,
the truth breaks open—your faithless heart
twisting what was ours into smoke,
a fragile dream you held only long enough to
shatter.

Once, your eyes were full of love for me.

Now they shine for her, so brilliant,

it's as if I've turned invisible. Can't you see? As
you hold her close, I disappear.

Broken fragments of my heart scatter,

crushed beneath the weight of lies

spread carelessly on the ground.

Watching you kiss her, I wonder—

did you ever love me?

Or was it all just pretend?

Now I see you clearly.

The ache that pierces me may soon fade.

For I know I deserve more

than to be treated as though I don't exist.

So I will leave you behind

and seek my treasure elsewhere—

with someone who will not crush my heart

the way you did.

Remembering You

Remembering you feels like running my fingers
across glass—

a fragile shimmer of beauty, edged with pain.

Once, life was soft in its colors, untouched by the
weight of the world.

Childhood was a dance in the sun,

laughter falling around me like golden leaves.

Innocence wrapped itself close,

a warm, familiar blanket.

I followed the wind eagerly,

every breath carrying the sweetness of flowers in
bloom.

The sky at dusk painted itself endlessly,

and I believed the days would last forever.

But those bright colors are tinged with sadness
now.

Shadows linger like ghosts, whispering lies

I can never quite escape.

Beyond that simple world,

my heart once knew no wounds,

no evil hiding in the corners.

Freedom's song drifted over fields of waving
grass,

and I was foolish enough to believe

life could always stay that good.

But those days slipped away—

like sand through my fingers beneath a burning
sun.

Now I remain a memory of the girl who once was
free,

longing for the simplicity that shines

like a distant star, trembling in the sky.

Haunted by the ache of all I've lost,

and yet—still reaching,

still reaching for that light.

Lost You

I missed you.

It wasn't loud—just a faint whisper,

yet it tore through me,

leaving an emptiness where warmth once lived.

The silence grew so heavy,

it pressed against my chest,

days dissolving into nights,

shadows crawling in as if they owned the world.

I barely recognized myself.

Each passing moment dragged at the edges of my
heart.

Hollow eyes stared back from the mirror,

haunted by memories that felt like they were
choking me.

And then it all collapsed.

Grief scattered me into fragments

I didn't know how to gather—

a storm I could never outrun.

But in the wreckage,

a spark flickered—

fragile, almost invisible,

yet enough to remind me

that hope, though buried, still breathes

Little by little, I began to feel again.

Memories rose from the cracks,

like wildflowers blooming where none should.

Yes, it hurt—

it hurt like hell—

but even pain carried a trace of beauty.

Finding myself again was not simple.

It was messy, brutal,

and unbearably slow.

Yet step by step,

I began to see her—

the girl I thought I'd lost forever.

Damaged, yes.

Bruised, of course.

But still here,

and stronger than I ever imagined.

Perhaps this is the nature of losing everything:

you uncover what remains—

and somehow,

that is enough.

Oceans Calling

In the depths of the ocean's affection,

within the heartbeat of the waves, I perceive a
goal—

a destination difficult to secure in our world.

The tides, which know no rest,

the sea, whose dance never ends,

remind me that we return to life in cycles,

just as dreams always recur.

The blue ocean's expanse,

the horizon stretching without limit,

serve as symbols of the boundless opportunities

hidden within us.

This is why I stand at the door of opportunity,

watching the ocean's majesty,

feeling the healing power of its embrace,

and whispering—thank you

for giving me a reason to live.

I am inspired, for now I see

that my path, too, can be found—

as if I were navigating life's course,

surfing upon destiny's billows.

So I begin my journey across the sea of purpose,

taking up the trials of the future,

guided by the wisdom of the sea,

which lends me strength everlasting.

In this moment, I feel whole and complete,

for it is then I know I exist

for a reason.

Just as the sea's vast and hidden bed

has no visible end,

so too is my intention—

boundless as the ocean's wilderness.

Secrets

The burden I bore in secret was jagged,

sharp and uneven.

Like splintered glass catching light,

it glittered merrily through the affliction.

From a distance, the smiles seemed flawless
illusions.

Yet, when looked at closely,

they revealed fissures, etched with a strange
tenderness.

I stitched myself together with strands of sorrow.

Each scar became a silver thread,

tracing my passage through this world of pain

toward a place better than yesterday.

And though broken, still I move on.

She saw beauty even in tongues

that wagged in poverty—

though everything else was falling apart.

Bread Ties

It was a rainy Tuesday.

You wrapped it around my finger,

your shiny eyes dancing

with the promise to replace it someday—

because you wanted forever

I looked at it and sighed:

green, twisted tight, secure,

just like I felt in your arms.

I wore it with pride for a year,

coated it in glitter to make it sparkle,

the way I sparkled in your eyes.

Funny, how much you held together

with a simple bread tie.

And how much could fade with growing up.

Eventually, like the tie, the promise unraveled.

But still—

I love rainy days.

Underwhelmed

I'm the woman who quietly holds up the world,

invisible beneath the crushing weight I carry for everyone else.

I stitch together their chaos,

smoothing the edges until I fade away.

And in the silence where thanks should live,

my heart aches—

a hollow reward for the love I pour into every task.

Yet still, I stand—longing to be seen,

waiting for gratitude that will never come.

Portrait

Their silence fills the house where love once
lingered.

I stand forgotten a portrait once treasured, now
drowning in dust.

I was a flower once deemed worthy of water;

now I wilt, roots dry but surely, they've just been
busy.

I am the tree they no longer bother with,

brittle, bare,

memories carved deep though I tell myself it's
unintentional.

My heart is a wasteland,

where even weeds have surrendered,

yet still it longs for the family

who vanished like a fading whisper.

I wander a lost child in the wreckage of their
indifference,

waiting for a hand I know will never return.

But still—

what's one more day?

Mirror

I was here with them a mirror cracked, losing its reflection.

Their words are ashes,

soft-spoken yet choking.

My smile a puppet molded from fragile mud and every nod a comfort

that wounds me gently,

like a bullet wrapped in silk.

I reach for their gentleness

like the last flicker of flame,

but only shadows gather in my hands.

What they took away, I hate them for—

those pieces of myself now gone.

Yet secretly,

I still lament for an unreturned love.

Wounded

Waves crash unrelenting,

carrying tides of uncertainty

across the vast shore of emptiness

where you've left me waiting for you.

I've been here so long,

my heart like driftwood porous, unfilled,

etched with the story of wear,

your version of love

eroding me grain by grain.

I wish you still saw me as the willow I once was,

dancing in the rain,

branches cascading with beauty,

drawing onlookers in

with a magic that was only mine.

I wish you knew me before the fractures,

before my branches broke,

before fear crept in,

before pain became my world.

I'd give anything to hold your gaze

the way other blooms do to linger in your mind
like a fragrance

that intoxicates,

like gardens that aren't mine.

I'd give anything for you to carve our initials

into the heart of my center,

and mean it with the core of you.

Action

Demons dance in plain sight.

They wear suits, kiss wives, cut ribbons—
community heroes,

so you never recognize their emptiness.

Some inspire, creating masterpieces

from the energy of unsuspecting traumas.

They mold darkness into light,

blinding the masses from seeing

the devil inside.

Their victims, too young to understand,

are sacrificed to the canvas

of sadistic energy now blazing across the screen,

a box-office hit,

infused with raped souls devoured.

Sometimes the quiet on set is deafening,

where spirits are broken more than legs,

and eyes are trained to turn blind.

There is no safety among the stolen and damned.

Stars are trapped in the darkness;

they never own their light.

Controlled, delivered entertainment for the
ignorant.

But still,

the show must go on.

Thoughts One

Life is full of idiosyncrasies, shaping the constant ebb and flow of emotion in all we do.

Each rise and fall of circumstance invites us to respond in kind, our emotions echoing the energy of our environment.

Yet, if we focus on what we can control our responses it becomes clear that we have the power to reshape the perspective we carry toward life's challenges

We hold the paintbrush that cascades color into the canvas of our lives.

And like all art, what becomes a masterpiece depends on the perspective of the viewer.

Change your perspective, change your response and you change your world.

Lost

I got lost in loving them,

repeating the move,

each time they left, I lost another piece of my soul.

I tried to fill the emptiness with fragments they left
behind—

not a whole, but scattered pieces,

traces woven through my life,

never able to come back together.

The more I tried to blend them into me,

the less of myself remained.

My face grew unfamiliar—

an open wound carved by their absence,

spread across every part of who I once was.

And then there was you.

Not in shining armor, not as a savior,

but as a solemn reminder of what I had been
missing within.

Without trying to fill the gap or mend me,

you simply stood there,

holding a mirror,

showing me the person, I had never seen before.

Though your presence was soft-spoken,

it felt like early morning light,

touching places in me I thought were gone.

So, I gathered myself bit by bit—

not from them,

but from the fragments I had forgotten

were always mine.

You did not rescue me—

I realized I did not need rescue.

In the empty spaces they left behind,

I planted my own seeds,

roots reaching deeper

than they could ever go.

And as I grew,

I no longer saw myself as broken,

but as something beautiful being remade.

It took your silent presence

to teach me how to love

the person I am becoming.

Childhood

A web of memories born from pain and struggle,

stitched with old wounds and tears—lies in the depths of my mind. And yet, in the end, I discovered courage: an inner strength that never fades.

Even when the flame feels small, it burns through every trial, through every heavy breath,

through the weight of a breaking heart. The journey was long, the path unforgiving

The journey was long; the path was difficult however every time I fell down only made me

grow higher than before with every tear that

tends to be a sharpened decision on my part that turns your grievances into power and your blemish into proof that you've managed to

overcome.

I stand now finishing this verse, battered and bruised yet unbroken, didn't become a

victim but emerged victorious over myself with all
my hurt still intact showing me what I am now

made of. And every mark bears witness while
every teardrop opens one's eyes further.

Strong when alone,

I am an example that through even the darkest

despair we still have light within ourselves to lead
others on the path to survival.

Twilight

Days dissolve into nights, nights collapse into days
and I remain, caught in a spider's web at dusk.
Neither moving forward nor falling back, I hang in
the half-light, suffocating beneath sparkling
delusions beautiful, yes, but empty of any future.
Suspended in a vacuum, adrift in aloofness, I no
longer feel with my soul. My heart is silent, my
spirit muted, as if I am only a machine running
endless routines, uncomprehending, protected or
imprisoned inside this hollow shell of solid iron.

Growth

A woman's journey is never still each step
reshaped by change,

her story sung in quiet echoes

until it blooms,

more radiant than before.

She spreads her wings wide,

emerging from the chrysalis

of who she once was.

Fear falls away,

replaced by a fragile hope

that spills from the soul like light.

Like a serpent shedding skin,

she sees with new eyes clear, unafraid.

Her song rings out,

bravery stitched into every note.

Rooted deep in the earth,

she still stands tall,

amused by the vastness of the universe.

Her posture is steady, her spirit unshaken.

Once she carried an old name,

now she writes her own a victor, not a victim.

And even when the rain comes,

she dances within it,

her laughter carrying through the air,

her soul taking flight.

A grown woman her story still untold,

yet already magnificent.

Loneliness

I long for something constant a love whose waves
are still, like water in a cloud:

gentle, unchanging, genuine, and pure.

To be loved without breaking,

even when the world is far from tranquil.

The world spins bright and noisy until I can't see
myself,

a story left unfinished, waiting for someone

to unfold the hidden parts of its script.

So I bide my time,

holding onto hope like a candle in the dark.

I dream of the one who will calm the night,

who will guide me to a place where peace feels
real.

What can I reach for, to feel true joy?

When that love arrives, it will be kind yet
unwavering,

like a light that shines even in shadow,

like a hand resting at the small of my back,

leading me toward brighter things.

For love does not only chase away darkness it
reshapes it,

turning shadow into peace.

And when it comes,

I will finally own it.

1

Regretting You

I have never found it simple to leave you.

The faint whispers of our love still resonate softly in my heart,

like lingering musical notes in the air notes, I cannot completely silence.

Yet I left a coward fleeing from the weight of my own fear.

A thousand doubts filled my mind, urging me to let go and move on.

I tore down the barriers you had built around your love,

and carried with me fragments of your faith,

believing those shattered pieces would help me rebuild myself.

I was foolish to think I could outrun the pain.

But with every step, the light grew dimmer,

62

and small fragments of joy slipped through my
hands,

until nothing was left to hold on to.

No, leaving you was never easy.

Even now, I am scattered—

a ghost of myself, fading in the glow of your love.

I kept reaching out to you,

only to discover you were no longer there.

And so, I found myself stranded among the ruins

of what we once were.

Nightfall

When all the stars, with their beauty and intrigue,

still leave me yearning,

I am accompanied only by the nostalgia

of your fingertips trailing down my cheek.

When the moon looks frostbitten

through the weary lenses of my swollen eyes,

the chill in the air cuts less than the coldness of
your heart,

as you stripped away my illusions of love's
security.

When the clouds resemble ashen fog,

breathing becomes shallow, still—

as your memory storms across my mind

like waves upon the sea,

drowning me in the whirlpool tides of your
indifference.

And when I am finally dragged to my knees by the darkness,

pain pressed firm against my chest, holding me in place,

only then does the goddess within my soul emerge,

teaching me once again how to love from within.

Aftermath

My life is the aftermath of a burn from a searing
kettle,

boiling with diluted illusions of once-vibrant
dreams.

The sting is gone now—nerves scorched,
unresponsive.

Only emptiness, in racing thoughts,

wraps around me in that familiar suffocating
embrace,

the one that has violated me so many times before.

What is this empty silhouette in the looking glass,

if not a reflection cast by the paradox that is me?

Always grasping for things imagined but never
definite,

no direction but a tumble—

a constant stumble, scraping exposed knuckles

against jagged shale.

I am cold, empty, forgotten.

And to remember how to feel

would still be nothing more

than vast, resounding nothingness within.

Dreaming

In a land of magic and mystery,

where moonlight enchants itself,

stars laugh with excitement,

and a love story begins.

Step by step, it guides our hearts—

a rhythm divine,

two beats aligned as one.

I crossed that bridge with you,

each step deepening our love

more and more.

We twirl beneath a sky of stars,

to the grand symphony of wind and trees.

Fireflies dance in joy,

celebrating a love untamed at heart.

We found our love in that enchanted place,

strong enough to heal every wound,

brave enough to chase away sorrow.

It welcomed us into its warm embrace

and carried us far beyond.

Now we stand together,

drawn into this land of enchanted love,

our hearts united for all time.

Our love eternal—

shining like the stars.

Inner Child

There are moments within the dreary shades of
every day,

when nostalgia sparks the senses

and the technicolor of childhood

flashes into the present.

When traumas fall silent

and anxiety gently dissipates,

when happiness feels innocent again—

untouched, unconditioned.

In these rare moments, the noise fades.

The mind surrenders its grip of tension

for the frayed ribbons of solace.

Here, in a place built for your inner child to play,

you can always hold a day pass to visit—

but never expect to stay.

For this place is woven from fragments of the past,

while the present is ever calling you forward.

Firsts

Butterflies dance gently, a flutter from within,

as lovers' lips

taste virgin skin.

Hearts ignite, passions new—

lucid wonderment, tender and true.

Wide-eyed pauses, smiles demure,

caressing lips

as hands seek more.

Eyes rivet, shining, reborn.

Innocence parts,

exalted passion now adorns.

Turbulence

Loving you was never easy.

The walls you built from past heartbreak

were like sharp rocks, tearing at my already
wounded heart.

But still, I climbed, driven by madness,

falling deeply under your enigmatic spell.

Your gaze held countless unspoken words,

calling to my soul, begging to be heard.

I attempted to scale the heights of your emotional
barrier,

leaving bits of myself behind, frayed by the harsh
realities

of your convoluted love.

With the remnants of my shattered self, I tried to
heal you,

foolishly believing that my sincere efforts could reach you.

But my own light diminished as I gave more of myself away,

not realizing there was a limit to how much I could give.

No, loving you was never straightforward.

And now I am left feeling lost, incomplete,

tumbling from the aftershocks of your bitter demeanor.

I can reach no further.

Bliss

Beneath the warm sun's embrace,

in the soothing whispers of the breeze,

I find a peace that eludes me

amid the rush of everyday life.

The rustle of leaves, the chirping of birds,

the gentle hum of nature's symphony

fills me with joy unbridled,

a happiness that is pure and true.

In the swaying of the trees, the flow of the river,

I see the rhythm of life itself—

a dance both serene and wild,

a force ancient and divine.

The scent of flowers, the touch of grass,

the taste of fresh air on my lips

remind me of the beauty that surrounds me,

the gift of nature that sustains me.

For in these moments of quiet contemplation,

I find a solace that is hard to find,

a reminder of the power of stillness,

the strength that comes from letting go.

And so I stand here, grateful and content,

in the embrace of nature's loving arms,

a happy soul at peace with the world,

bathed in the light of nature's purest charms.

Enchanted

There is magic where the stars kiss the Earth,

in a place where fireflies dance on moonbeams,

and trees gossip quietly with the winds.

A solitary bridge spans a hazy stream,

its waters a mixture of dreamers' reality,

shimmering with the wishes of souls yearning.

It is in this sanctuary that my heart's essence called
for you,

sending my blind desire across the currents of
time,

seeking the matching beat to my unique rhythm.

Fragile in my vulnerability,

you surfaced like a shooting star amidst the naivety
of my world.

How simply complex it is to love and be loved,

to reach love's center, her core, and drift within her
currents.

Remember

The moment I swung from the trees,

my face lifted to meet the sun's kiss,

my cheeks burning scarlet at your first glance.

I felt your danger before I knew your name.

The carefree intensity of your gaze staggered my
breath—unapologetically,

intrusively, invading my mind,

where once unicorns danced

and ballerinas grew dizzy in their infinite grace.

Your smirk made me reckless in my intrigue.

In that moment, in my garden,

I passed through the gate into the unknown.

My butterflies followed, nesting in my abdomen,

fluttering in a frenzy as your fingertips lit my skin,
conflagrant,

wrapping my heart in an unfamiliar cocoon

of love's chaotic beauty.

Borderline Ride

Between the panic attack and the breakdown,

somewhere after my mind has racked my body

with emotions larger than the ocean,

causing tides of exhaustion.

After I experience bliss in extremes

and despair with the next trigger,

before I hate you, when I really hate me,

the only constant I have remains my love for
you— acting like a lighthouse,

unmoving in the storms of my trauma,

making me believe

I can heal and find the horizon again.

Thoughts Two

I am the mosaic they don't understand,

fractured edges sharp enough to draw blood, yet
gleaming in the light of what's left of me.

In a world that worships perfection, I am chaos too
jagged to fit, too raw to be swallowed whole.

They avert their eyes from my scars, my ruins,

yet I stand unashamed,

a masterpiece carved from wreckage.

I am not what they want,

but I am everything they fear a reminder that
beauty can survive the breaking.

Growing Paints

Mix my colors with precision,

a scientist at work in my small studio.

A scent hangs in the air, intoxicating in its chaotic
aroma.

Embers smolder amid the ashes of self-doubt.

Oh, how fickle a shade!

Tattered remnants of a soul once whole,

staggered dreams beaten into submission by the
very obstacles that keep me down.

I wish I were the masterpiece rather than the
sketch you see me as.

How I have always longed for you to close your
eyes and envision me.

I get it, though—the sketch is incomplete, yet
always growing,

despite the blatant imperfections.

The masterpiece is erratic in its beauty, but still sought after.

Oh, to be the paint.

My Mind

Fractured soul, tormented in a kaleidoscope of perspectives.

The colors of emotion often blur the lines of reality.

Oh, how the constant coil of life changes the arrays, mocking in their reflection the beauty just out of reach.

Fragments remain to cast a picture of feigned perfection.

Dancing among the shards, unique in a chaotic rhythm, amplified by the light, haunted by the shadows born from ruination.

Motherless Child

Plenty lay claim to a child, to a name bright as the
sun, with tears sharp as the rain.

Each time they "loved" her, it only added to the
pain,

misunderstood, then forgotten.

"She's too much to handle, she drives me insane!"

Words that cut to the core, no cure, no refrain.

Sparkling eyes dulled, made hard,

the scraps of supposed love leaving innocence
scarred.

Madness turned to rage, and rage to regret,

every memory becoming impossible to forget.

As the child grew, lost to affection in her world,

full of selfish intent unfurled by others,

out of sight, out of mind—the safest way to
sustain.

She ran far away to keep herself sane.

No more false love, no more pretending to "care."

She knew deep down, they hated her there.

Fake hugs and kisses, obligatory love these are things of her past.

Thank the graces above.

And God finally showed her how to heal her tattered heart.

He gave her true love, an amazing life start,

staring up at her with sparkling eyes.

She saw the innocence before all the lies.

She cried tears of joy, for she finally knew

she was loved completely and rewarded for all she had endured.

And for those left behind, weighed down by self-centered stress,

who attempted to harm a child they could not comprehend:

May God shine a light on you, so you understand

a child is an innocent soul who needs your hand.

Without you, they may be lost—but not for long,

because God writes the words to a lonely child's
song.

Within those words lie the lessons lacking

from those who fail to nurture, who neglect their
part.

So stop focusing on yourself and your drama.

Rise up and become a phenomenal parent,

a loving Daddy, a devoted Mommy, an Uncle, a
Friend, or a Foster you matter more than you
know.

Do not become an imposter.

Smiles

You smile and say, "I love you."

I smile back, demurely,

knowing it's what is expected.

When did we, as women, learn these things?

To cater to the expectations of a love

and forsake the expectations of ourselves?

Your hands find my hips, your mouth, my lips,

and I surrender,

my mind wandering how long it will take before

I can pretend you lit me up, so your psyche isn't broken,

because mine is already shattered.

It's not you; in another world,

you would have been my compass.

Afterburn

After the sting, after the tears, after the yelling and
the whys. After the soul crumbles and the heart
cries, after you're too weak to stand and too tired
to sleep, and you can't decipher if you've eaten
this week.

When you don't know your next move, and your
security is shredded, and the demons are dancing
again, while you reel inside your head.

And the loneliness creeps in, and reality destroys
the dreams, and you can't stop remembering

all the promises broken amidst your own screams.

Only then do you see it, buried in debris,

tiny as an ember the emergence of thee.

She's fragile and sore, carrying all the pain so
long, but she smiles and nods knowingly.

And together you climb toward being strong,

and before long, the darkness fades.

And the sting becomes another scar,

and the pain turns to power,

when you learn to love who you are.

Self-Imagery

One day I woke up and I saw her, in mesmerizing
clarity. She shone from within, like a galaxy buried

within her breast. Her eyes sparkled with
happiness, illuminating her face

like microalgae across an empty shore.

Her body moved with an ease of comfort

that changed how she walked.

A gentle sway replaced the gaze she once held

fixed only on her feet,

and her shoulders rested back with confidence.

She smiled at me, a knowing secret on her lips,

and for the first time since I could remember,

I loved the image in that old, floor-length mirror.

Femininity

The complexity of womanhood—

is it a subject of endless debate?

To bloom in grace, to charm, to satisfy,

to shine despite the rage within.

To heal when you are the victim of another's sin,

smile through masked tears, stay driven through

fear. To be strong, tough, and chic,

but not so much that a man feels threatened by his

own insecurities. You offend him with your

mystique.

Fading

Feelings fade like the thread in those jeans that fit
just right. Like your hand used to fit in mine,

until you stopped reaching for it. The distance in
one room became a rigid canyon

between our bodies. I remember falling asleep on
the phone, when our voices were lullabies to our
souls, when every night we spent entangled in each
other's scent, not to be let go until sunrise.

There was a time when our kisses could make
storybooks jealous. Now, they've been replaced by
forced pecks of indifference

But though our lights dim, my heart still quietly
calls for you. I just wish you were still listening.

Thoughts Three

Loving him was like holding onto smoke—
beautiful and fleeting, but never mine to keep.

His touch, though tender, always felt borrowed; his
smile, a shadow of something I could never fully
claim.

I saw it in his eyes—that quiet ache for a life he
would never share with me—

the way his love lingered just out of reach, settling
like dust instead of fire.

And yet, I stayed, clinging to the scraps,

until the weight of knowing I would always be
"enough for now"

crushed the fragile dream of what we could have
been.

First Love

At first, I wasn't looking for love.

I wanted no part in my life,

for I had surrendered to the vast void of hope.

All I wanted was to hide within my own

hollowness. Then, for just an instant, a spark of

change you provoked a chance,

breached my curtain wall,

catapulting my heart into a dance.

I never fathomed, nor put much stock in,

finding someone offering a heart so pure and sure

the friend who became a lover, all one could ever

pray for. A mystery to finally count on, to listen

and understand, a lover to hold onto,

one who protects my soul within his hand.

My heart ignites at your smile, especially when it

is true,

and my world, once cold, empty, and void,

awakens an Eden of possibility,

designed by fate… for you.

Hopeful

I lay awake at night,

imagining what we'd be like

without the barriers

built by scorned lovers past. Would we dance

in a rhythm all our own? Or would the insecurities

of reminiscent bruises cause our feet to stumble?

I ponder the sincerity behind our kisses—

warm and unwary. Or do we remain fixed at the

shore, fear-stricken by the depths of it all?

How I long to drown in the complexity of your

love, to emerge on the surface, gasping in

wondrous exhilaration,

diving deeper into the depths of your world.

Your surface glimmers, oh so inviting,

sending waves of intrigued enticement

to tickle my soul as I gaze in silent amazement and
intimidation

at the vastness that encompasses you.

How dare you invade my solace so?

With your cool yet unavoidable charms,

pulling me slowly toward the deepness,

where I must trust that you will hold safe

my heart, tattered and unable to float.

Drown me, gently sweet love, for your sea is
dangerous, and I am yet still too weak to hold my
poise against the feelings stirring in the deepest
shadows of the moonlight you reflect effortlessly.

If I must sink in love, conquered and stripped to
the very center of all that I am,

let it be you who shows me the beauty in the
darkness.

Let it be you who gives me your breath,

that I may remain submerged and tranquil

within your mystery.

Make me forget that empty, haunting shore,

for it is a place I do not wish to return to.

Take me deep, and protect me

until we both forget the demons

that held us back from living.

Sisterhood

If only you knew me,

when my smile was still innocent,

when my laugh came from my heart and my eyes
still reflected my soul. I was a dream.

Before the "I dos," when I lived my life by the
rising of the sun, not the nuisance of an alarm,

when I met my needs with every note I listened to,

every cruise with a boy, and every butterfly that
rose in my tummy—

back when I was free, when I was me.

Time has a way of taming our wildness with
others' needs,

and love makes us give selflessly, dutifully,
silently,

until we are a ghost of our truth.

However, all is never lost.

Sometimes a ray of sunshine, so blinding,

can protrude from the cloud bank of the mundane

and be so stunning and pure that we feel her again.

And the forced smile becomes true once more.

Twin Flames

We were always meant to be, two halves of the same destiny.

Our hearts beat as one, our souls ignite, a love that's pure, a love that's bright. Our journey may be long and tough, but together, we are strong enough.

We'll face the storms, we'll brave the pain,

for our love—it will always remain.

We were born from the same flame, twin flames, forever the same. Our love is a fire that never dies,

a burning passion that lights up the skies.

We are each other's missing part,

two hearts that beat as one, a work of art.

Our love is a river that flows so deep, a bond unbroken, a promise to keep.

Together, we'll conquer every fear,

together, our love will always be here.

For we are twin flames, meant to be,

a love that will last eternally.

Rambles

Compelling thoughts twist the mind,

shredding the flesh of the subconscious rind.

Words to paper, less to hear,

ink to page, condemned to love laced in fear.

Tremble within as truth burns,

fresh tears fall like ash against the flesh.

Suffocating silences surround the screaming soul,

impending sadness exacts its toll.

The mind laughs, mocking the foolish heart,

the heart defiant, loathing the mind from the start.

And Time, ever patient, watches each tear

as it rips the soul apart.

Rediscovery

I found myself in the spaces you left behind—

pieces I didn't even know were missing.

When you were gone,

the silence was so loud that it forced me to listen.

And that's when it began:

—the slow, painful work of finding out who I

really am.

Letting go of the person your love shaped me into

wasn't easy,

but it gave me room to grow.

Like a seed breaking through the soil, I stretched

toward something bigger, something that was mine

alone.

Emerging opportunities beckoned me to stand

independently,

to see that I was enough all along.

The chains of our past finally fell away when I
chose to stop holding on to what couldn't stay.

In the freedom that followed, I began to love

myself not because of you,

but because of what I found after you.

I stopped chasing approval from those who
couldn't see me.

The realization of my worth had always been
waiting to be claimed. Now, I'm piecing myself
back together, slowly but surely.

I'm no longer afraid to stand tall.

I know who I am, and I am proud of her.

It wasn't easy, but I feel whole now—

free from the weight of everything that once held
me back.

I walk forward, not because I have to,

but because this path is mine.

And as I move, I reach for the stars,

untethered and unafraid.

Riptide

Dreams are dangerously delicious.

To have them is to hold hope.

To fail to obtain them is to live in wanting.

To stand stalled on the shores of chance,

never risking the brackish pools of potential
swirling around you.

To be pulled by the allure of their wonder,

yet held back by the anxious winds of embedded
trauma.

The sheer terror and exhilaration of freefall are
ever present.

To witness others, move with ease in their skiffs of
faith,

sailing toward the horizon of promise,

adds weight to the anchor of sadness wrapped tight
around your soul.

The ropes remain taut and binding, holding you in
envy.

Do you think, when they hurt you, they realized
they condemned you—

to remain a lighthouse on the shore,

never crossing the break into tomorrow?

Absence

I lie beside him—

the sheets vast chasms, cold and unyielding.

His warmth, a memory: flickering, fading, always
just out of reach.

Once, his touch painted constellations,

a galaxy mapped across my skin.

Now his hands rest like stone—still, foreign,

unfamiliar in their silence.

I whisper his name into the void between us,

but the shadows swallow my voice.

He doesn't hear me. He never hears me.

Smiles, fractured performances.

Intimacy, my grand façade.

Love, the stage I tread alone.

The absence of passion mocks me—

an ache sharpened by the memory of fire.

Am I the ghost,

a remnant of what we were, haunting the ruins of

us?

Or is he the specter, drifting further

into the hollow echo of apathy?

And still, I remain,

dancing in the fragments,

cut by the shards of what once burned.

longing for the flames that will never return.

Hindsight

I was born in hand chains, not metal ones.

Rough hands stole my name, humiliated me, and

left me hollow—

sustenance only for their hunger.

They shattered the core of who I was.

Darkness smothered my screams, and their words

cut like knives,

leaving me voiceless.

Yet even then, something inside me held on—

a resilient spark, fighting to survive in the ashes.

I clawed my way out, flesh torn, scars blazing.

I rose from my rage and stood tall.

Their fire forged the blade, sharper, stronger than

the original.

Though the shadows linger,

I no longer fear them.

I have become storm and fire—

unbreakable, unshattered.

Full Circle

I was their shadow, a stolen breath,

folded into corners

where no one dared to look.

Hands like claws,

tearing pieces of me a child turned currency

for monsters cloaked in power.

I learned to scream in silence,

to vanish while standing still,

to survive in fragments.

They built empires on my shattered soul,

but even in the dark, I burned.

They thought I was theirs but you cannot own

what refuses to die. I rose, jagged and relentless, a

storm born of their ruin.

Now I hunt them drag them into the light,

tear their masks to dust. For every child they broke, I am vengeance. For every life they stole, I am wrath. They made me prey, but I became their judge.

Birth

I became that child of nowhere—

thrown aside, neglected,

only words carried in the wind.

Love did not compute.

It was an abstract word,

a haunting more than a comfort.

The years dragged long and harsh.

My heart, battered and broken,

beat like an irregular drum.

Each crack a scar from a hand that turned away.

Then you appeared—vulnerable, ageless—

a warmth that shadows had never dared to reach.

Your very first wail sang to me

a chorus of belonging.

The tones of completeness

swept away my frosty hiss.

From you—fragile, with your small hands—

I drew new power

I never knew still ran within me.

They flung me to the ends of the earth,

yet you never stopped loving me.

You were an ocean,

carrying me back to myself.

Because love means creating something new

without considering oneself.

And you—

you are the living fire of it.

You burn brighter

than any darkness they ever brought.

Irony

They tell us to be rivers—

soft enough to glisten in sunlight,

yet strong enough to carve stone.

To flow gently,

never spilling too far.

Strength is radiant, they say,

when it hides beneath a smile—

a quiet resilience,

never loud, never unruly.

Be the bloom they admire,

but never let the petals fall.

Carry the weight of storms,

yet stay delicate in the breeze.

Strong and soft,

like a ribbon in the wind—

bound tightly,

but graceful in its flight.

Cynder Girl

I am the tether he never wanted,

the thread binding him to a life

he never truly chose.

His promises—spoken like offerings—

now feel like chains,

rusting under the weight of his regret.

I see it in the way his shoulders bow,

as though the very air suffocates him.

His eyes wander past me,

past this home we built brick by brick,

searching for her—

a ghost made of smoke,

a dream he can never quite forget,

even as I stand here, flesh and bone.

He stays, but his love is a dimming candle,

its flame flickering,

its warmth fading with each passing day.

Every "I love you" is a quiet surrender,

a whisper meant for the life

he might have lived instead.

And I—his reason, his regret, his ruin—

carry his reluctant devotion

like a stone in my chest,

aching beneath the weight of knowing

I am not the fire he wanted,

but the ember he cannot leave.

Kaleidoscope

I turn the kaleidoscope of us,

twisting it slowly, watching the shards scatter.

Amber laughter, cerulean tears,

frosted memories of quiet nights—

all falling apart.

The light hits differently now,

casting patterns I no longer recognize.

What was once soft and whole

is now sharp and uneven,

the place where love used to live.

Your name lingers in the glass,

a faint echo caught in reflection,

fractured into pieces

I cannot fit back together.

The promises we made flash like prisms,

splintering into truths I once refused to see.

Their jagged edges cut deep,

scarring the fabric of memory.

I thought we were forever—unchanging, constant,

our colors mapped like constellations.

But even stars collapse under their own weight.

And we too fell—

beautiful, shattering,

like a meteor streaking across a lonely sky.

Now I turn the kaleidoscope alone,

watching the chaos settle into something new.

The patterns aren't perfect—

strange, uneven—

but in their broken beauty,

I see a faint glimmer of hope.

Maybe not everything needs to fit together

to still be worth holding onto.

Thoughts Four

I am like the wilted flower,

turning toward a sun

that has already distanced itself.

It feels almost poetic—

how I keep reaching for warmth,

knowing the season

has already changed.

Bouquet

Petals curl, brittle and worn,

their colors faded as time drifts away.

They once reached for the sun—

fearless, full of life—

but even the most radiant flowers

grow old, slowly.

The stems weaken, bowed

by the ancient weight the earth requires.

With the gentlest pull,

they hint at renewal.

Decay, however fraught with sorrow,

still holds its truth:

a letting go of what no longer serves,

a returning to ground and soil,

the source of all new growth.

I am like that flower—

drooping in loss and death,

scattering across the earth's floor.

Yet even as I fall,

my edges fading,

my roots reach deeper into the earth,

drawing new life from broken things.

It is here my growth takes place—

not as before,

but as something else.

Delicate, yet strong-willed,

waiting for the right time.

Tremors

I rose from the aftershock,

my fractures no longer cracks

but seams of gold—

the story of my survival stitched in light.

Every scream they silenced

became a thread in my tapestry.

Every weight they chained to me

forged me into glass—

once fragile, now tempered, unbreakable.

I am no longer dust beneath their feet.

I am the storm that reshaped the mountain,

the roots that split the pavement wide,

opening the earth

so others may bloom.

Settling

Smiled at, but never lingered on—

I am the girl,

the warmth tucked quietly somewhere in the room.

A light soft enough to edge the night,

but never dazzling enough to blind.

"Cute"—that is what they call me,

as though it were a prize to be won,

a bribe to keep me from wanting more.

Their eyes slide past me,

reaching for others with sharper lines,

faces carved by symmetry,

while I remain pliable earth,

shaped by gentle words.

Sometimes I am what they want for a night,

their steady stream of worshippers.

I am the soothsayer who knows their hearts,

haunting every image that resembles me.

Yet they say my value

is measured by appearance.

But what glitters in their eyes

cannot be seen by any but mine:

the fire that warms,

the voice that halts,

a heart too full

for their little world.

Wide Space

The fields stretch wide—

a golden sea beneath my fingertips,

the gentle wind a song only I can hear.

I have tasted the bitterness of storms,

felt their sharp edges pierce my core.

But here, it is different.

The air is sweet with wildflowers and fresh earth,

the soil soft and cool beneath my hand—

each seed slipping through my fingers

like a whispered promise of tomorrow.

From afar, the creek hums its clear, unbroken tune,

a reminder that life flows steadily, faithfully on.

The sun caresses my skin,

its warmth seeping through every layer,

pulling me deeper into its serene embrace.

I breathe in this living essence,

so richly simple,

and for the first time, I feel complete:

the scent,

the touch,

the sound—

a small, endless world within my hands.

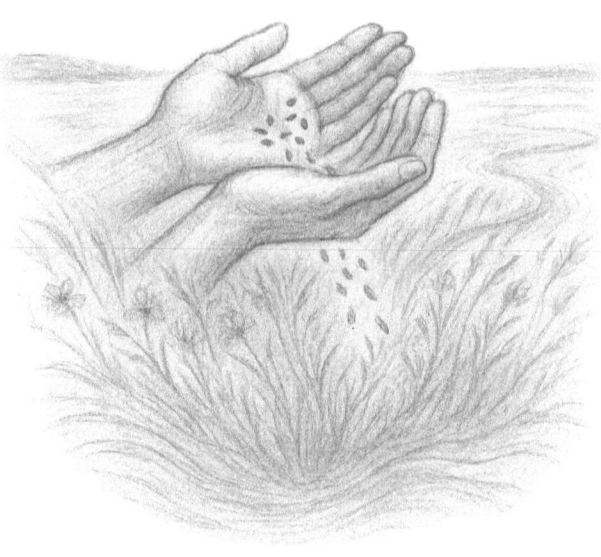

Life

To the shore, the tide murmurs vague secrets,

striving to return me to what I once was.

There was a time when I was a young girl—

a wild thing who danced in the waves,

believing they would never let me go.

Back then, the water was sweet on my skin,

not the salt that later turned to poison.

Every piece of the past moves within me,

lit by the glow of first loves,

already betrayed before I even understood.

The castles I built on sand were fragile,

washed away by rains I thought I could ignore.

That girl vanished, carried off with the tide.

In her place stands a woman,

bent beneath the weight of wounds she never asked

for.

Now the sun presses heavier—

not just warm, but sacred in its touch.

The breeze has lost its gentleness,

scratching blunt truths onto the places

where I was once soft.

Behind me, distorted grooves trace my stumbling

steps,

until the water rises, erasing my history.

And yet, the soil remains—

something I can still hold,

cupped carefully in both my hands.

It feels as if every grain carries a tale,

a scar etched deep in memory.

It is all about me now—

the dreamer, the shattered one,

yet still whole.

The ocean shaped me,

and I emerged sharp but true—

an edge too cutting to hold,

yet too radiant to turn away from.

Mindful

I wander through an enchanted glade,

where emotions sprawl like riotous ivy—

vivid, serrated,

a mosaic of brilliance that refuses to rest.

The air thrums with an electric pulse,

the ground quivers beneath my feet—

a labyrinth of wonder and turbulence,

both intoxicating and cruel.

My heart flutters like a moth to unseen light—

erratic, consuming, impossible to hold.

Love here is a tempest in amber,

captivating in its glow,

only to dissolve into vapor,

leaving behind the ache of hollow fire.

The trees murmur riddles I cannot solve,

their roots twisting through my thoughts.

Joy bursts like gilded embers—alive, consuming—

until shadows rise to drink it dry,

a cycle too relentless to outrun.

But in this glade, I am alive—

more alive than the world dares to be.

I blaze with the magic of it:

the jagged edges, the fleeting sparks,

the raw, untamed splendor of a soul

that feels everything

too brightly to be contained.

In Progress

My mind is a canvas stretched taut,

its surface a collision of unruly strokes—

vivid, ungoverned,

a cacophony of beginnings that refuse resolution.

Colors erupt in frenetic bursts,

each hue colliding with the next,

a restless choreography of thought

never quite aligned.

The brush hesitates, then lunges—

too many choices, too many paths.

Every line fracture,

every intention dissolve,

splintering into erratic forms,

patterns unraveling before they cohere.

Concepts flare at the edges of reason,

brilliant yet ephemeral,

slipping away like light through fissures.

I grasp at fragments—

ideas half-born, visions half-finished—

only to find my hands

ink-stained but empty.

And still, in the turbulence,

something visceral stirs.

The chaos breathes,

pulses with its own defiant rhythm—

a composition alive,

unrestrained by convention.

Though no steady hand could claim it,

this canvas speaks in motion—

in vibrancy, in imperfection,

140

in a mind unbound by rigid lines.

Incomplete, yes—

but infinite in its possibility.

Its beauty is etched

in the defiance of being tamed.

Reason

My heart became the moment he cried—

a sound so soft, yet vast, divine."

His fingers curled, impossibly small, and in that
instant, his soul held mine. The stars could shatter,
the skies unravel, the earth could tremble, the seas
be torn, yet he, my wonder, my endless light, is
why my spirit was ever born.

Through restless storms, through weight of
shadow, through trials that darken the brightest
day,

I marvel at him, my greatest creation,

a love no force could steal away. And though the
years may carry him far to places unknown where
dreams take flight,

I will love him still, with infinite awe:

my son, my miracle, my heart's pure light.

What's Missing

I came from roots that could never hold,

planted in soil too shallow to grow.

Their love was water that slipped away—

always out of reach,

leaving me parched for something real.

My childhood drifted like a leaf in the wind,

aimless, untethered,

where hands promised warmth

but never lingered long enough to keep me safe.

And then you came—

soft as a whisper,

small enough to fit perfectly

into the cracks of my fractured soul.

You were my light, my hope,

the answer to prayers I didn't know I'd spoken.

For a moment, I believed I could be enough—

enough to fill you with love so vast

it would eclipse the ache of my past.

I held you close, committing every detail of you to

memory:

the curve of your cheek, the weight of your breath,

the way your tiny fingers gripped mine

as though you were anchoring me to the earth.

But love is deeper than desire.

Love is the art of knowing when to release,

like setting free a cherished bird to soar.

And each step I took away

shattered my heart into irreparable pieces,

resonating with the pain of leaving. But in that

breaking, I poured every ounce of love I had into

you.

I placed you into arms I will never know,

praying they are softer, stronger—

praying they will cradle you

the way I always dreamed of being held.

I kissed your forehead,

pressing my love into your skin,

a quiet promise that I will never stop loving you.

I hope you grow in a world

where the sun shines without shadows,

where hands reach for you with care,

and where love feels safe, steady, and endless.

You are my heart, my reason,

the one I chose to give a life better than I ever had.

And if my name ever feels like a distant echo,

know this: you were never forsaken.

My love will always cradle you, even from afar.

You were loved so fiercely,

I broke myself open—

just to make sure you'd bloom.

Crumbs

You give me scraps

and call them love.

I, starving,

pretend they're enough.

Your touch—

a fleeting ghost.

Your words—

a knife wrapped in silk.

Still, I stay,

clinging to shadows,

terrified of the void your absence would leave—

even as you vanish,

piece by piece.

How long

can I survive

on the echo of you?

Again

We stand at the edge of this—

your arms reaching for me

as if they can erase the times, they let me fall.

You say it's different now,

but the silence between us burns

with the weight of all you've done.

You offer me moments of light:

a soft laugh,

a careful touch,

the way you say my name

like it's sacred.

And for a heartbeat,

I want to believe you.

But the cracks are everywhere—

in your voice,

in your gaze,

in the way you hesitate,

still clinging to secrets

I fear to find.

I am trying to love you

as if the past doesn't haunt me,

as if forgiveness could bind the wounds

you once left open.

But every word is a gamble,

every embrace an unspoken question:

will you stay whole this time,

or shatter me again?

This love feels like a battle

I am too tired to fight,

yet too desperate to surrender.

I stay,

because I need to believe

you can be better—

that we can be more

than the wreckage you left of us.

But love shouldn't feel like this:

gripping broken glass

and calling it hope.

I want to trust you,

but the urgency in my chest

screams louder than your promises.

And I don't know

how much longer

I can bleed for you.

Becoming

I stand on the cusp of myself—

a life unlearned,

built on service and silence,

now splintering into something new.

The world feels too vast,

my tools too small—

no letters behind my name, no map to follow,

only the weight of a past

I was never meant to escape.

But I have forged resilience

in the fire of others' needs,

shaped patience into steel,

turned sacrifice into strength.

This is not starting over—

it is becoming.

Fear clings like a shadow,

but so does hunger:

to own my name,

to rewrite my story,

to prove I was always enough.

The Greatest Cure

A pill silences the body's screams, smothers pain
beneath a chemical haze,

yet leaves the soul untouched raw, aching in places
medicine cannot reach. But nature, ancient and
unyielding, knows how to cradle a wounded spirit.

The wind doesn't mask your sorrow it carries it,

whispering through trembling leaves until the ache
softens.

Rain falls like absolution,

each drop dissolving the weight you've carried too
long. The ocean sings its boundless hymn, waves
crashing through memories

you thought would never release. The forest speaks
in symphonies, its shadows holding you gently, its
sunlight threading through branches

to show you the fractures

where the light gets in.

There is no side effect to birdsong, no hollow

numbness in the smell of earth after a storm. Here,

every sound, every scent, every breath of wild air

is a balm for wounds too deep for science to find.

Modern medicine tries to forget pain,

but nature teaches us to feel it to hold it, to release

it,

to begin again.

The Artist Heart

An artist wields the stroke—each line a scar laid
bare,

each color a memory unearthed. The canvas
becomes a mirror,

reflecting truths too jagged for words to hold.

It is creation through destruction—

a breaking open to let light in.

A musician paints differently, their canvas made of
air,

notes stretching across silence like a horizon.

Each sound layers itself, a landscape unfolding—

not with the sharp edges of pain, but with the soft
embrace of something whole.

The artist cuts into the fabric of suffering, tearing
images from the dark,

while the musician gathers what remains, offering

shape to chaos,

form to the formless.

The brush demands confrontation: Look at what

you've endured.

The notes invite renewal: Feel what you've

become.

To be both—

to paint with strokes and sound,

to draw from agony and weave harmony—

is to live within the duality of creation:

to know the masterpiece comes only

from the weight of ruin, the grace of healing, and

the infinite love carried in every breath.

Alchemy

Suffering carves with brutal precision, each wound

a chisel against the soul,

etching truths too jagged for joy to ever hold. The

more you fracture,

the sharper the vision—

a violent grace in the way pain pulls beauty from

the ashes.

Joy is fleeting, featherlight, its hues too shallow

to stain the canvas deeply.

But pain—

pain paints in relentless strokes,

its shadows shifting like storm clouds, colliding

and breaking,

revealing slivers of light only the broken can see.

It terrifies,

this truth that gnaws at the bone: only in ruin

does creation rise, only through despair does art

find its voice.

Suffering is both fire and forge,

consuming what you were

to shape what you will become—

turning agony into something too vivid for silence.

Fractured

Fractured, never meant to thrive here—on the

precipice of desolation,

where frost sculpts stone and the wind's howl

erodes resolve.

The world bore down,

its frigid insistence unrelenting,

even my own reflection

murmured defeat:

You are not enough.

Yet my roots infiltrated fissures, staking claim to

the inhospitable.

I drew strength from resistance—each petal an

assertion,

each thorn a warning:

I will endure.

A rose born of defiance,

I flourish where statistics forbid—

a rebellion etched deep

into the marrow of the mountain.

Fake Mourning

They cried for me once wet eyes, trembling voices, a grief so convincing it almost fooled me. For a moment, I believed the world cared.

But their tears dried before the news cycle did, and I became nothing more than a headline skimmed, then forgotten.

They lit their candles, whispered their prayers, and called it enough. They painted themselves as saviors while the wolves still prowled, still fed on children like me.

Their hands never turned a lock, never ripped the shadows apart. They left us there. I was only a number to them a tragedy for their guilt, never their action.

They didn't search for me. They didn't fight for me. They whispered never again, but they lied. They always lie.

I know what they are the quiet accomplices,

the ones who look away,

who call silence mercy

and inaction safety.

They let it happen

because it was easier than fixing it.

But I'm still here.

And I'm furious.

I clawed my way out,

dragging every scar with me.

They didn't save me.

No one saved me.

And that fire in me it burns hotter now.

For every child they left behind, for every door
they never opened,

for every tear they shed

just to be seen.

They will feel this fire.

They will learn what it means

to face the fury of someone

they forgot to bury

Thoughts Five

Becoming a mother felt like regrowing roots

where mine had once been torn away.

My mother who chose me but never stayed—

taught me nothing of love,

only how easily it can be abandoned.

She planted me in her garden and left:

the soil dry,

the promise of care a lie.

Her absence carved a scar that never faded,

her betrayal a storm that hollowed me out.

But even in the void, I made a vow:

I will not be her.

Every cry I soothed was defiance,

every small hand I held a reminder

that love is kept, not claimed.

Her neglect became my blueprint in reverse,

her silence the ground I overturned

to plant something unshakable.

I stayed where she ran,

gave where she withheld,

loved where she abandoned.

And in my children's laughter,

I built the home she refused to be.

Quicksand

She skips the hopscotch of chaos,

her heart a gilded furnace—

too soft for the edges it has known.

Borderlines carve her,

sharpening every breath

into a question of survival.

The ground beneath her shifts,

sinking under the weight of herself,

yet she learns to clutch at fleeting moments,

to hold on just long enough

to imagine something steady.

Her mind is a battlefield,

her body a vessel of contradictions—

fragile and furious,

aching for something real.

She is not whole,

but she is relentless:

an unsteady force

chasing the promise of solid ground.

Gracing Myself

The stray hairs that frame my face, are unruly,

but soft in the morning light.

The quiet pride in bare skin,

scarred, glowing, and mine alone.

The way my hands feel against cool earth,

nails unpolished,

but strong enough to nurture innocence.

A laugh that escapes too loudly, the warmth in my

cheeks

when I catch my own reflection— not flawless,

but real,

and enough.

It's these cherished moments, unadorned,

imperfect,

that remind me being a woman

is its own kind of amazing.

Mans Silence

I see it in his eyes—

the quiet erosion of a soul

bearing burdens unspoken.

The world presses down,

unyielding,

demanding resilience

yet denying him the grace of fragility.

His words falter, caught in his throat,

fears and failures buried deep

beneath the armor he was told to wear.

No one asks how it feels to break

when he is expected to remain unbroken.

From here,

it is a tragedy in slow motion—

the steady drowning of a man clinging to silence,

grasping at pride

as if it's the only thing keeping him afloat.

And I wonder:

what cruel design taught him

that strength is solitude,

that vulnerability is weakness?

What will it take for him to see

that the strongest men

are those who know

when to let themselves fall?

Withered

I have stood through centuries,

my roots tangled in the earth's marrow,

my branches clawing at the heavens.

Storms have roared against my bark,

lightning has split my limbs,

yet none of it rivals

the destruction they wield against their own.

I watch them—

their sharp edges,

their barbed words slicing deeper

than any axe they've driven into me.

They move like fire,

devouring what they touch,

leaving ash in their wake—

scarred soil,

broken bonds,

silence heavy with regret they'll never speak
aloud.

They pause beneath my shade,

eyes lifted to the canopy

as if seeking absolution,

as if my stillness holds

the answers they cannot bear to hear.

But their glances are fleeting,

their hands brutal,

their footsteps pressing wounds

into the earth they claim to love.

And I want to scream:

Growth demands care.

Strength lives in the intertwining.

Not in the severing.

But I have no voice—

only the ache of rings etched by their wars.

I am rooted in their ruin,

my leaves trembling

at the violence they call survival.

All I can do is stand,

a witness to their cruelty,

waiting for the day

they remember how to grow

without destruction.

Littles

My love for you is spun sugar—

a dream stitched with sweetness,

like cotton-candy clouds

and honey-soaked laughter, soft and endless,

melting into every moment we share.

It floats like bubbles, weightless and magical,

rising with every breath you take,

glistening in colors the sun painted just for you.

Each carries my wishes, my hopes,

my quiet, unspoken prayers for your happiness.

At night, it glows like moonlight,

a silken thread of silver

woven gently through your dreams.

It wraps around you, soft as stardust,

whispering love into the quiet,

keeping you safe in its eternal glow.

You are my wonder,

my light,

my sweetest dream made real.

And my love for you

will forever be sugar on the breeze,

bubbles in the air,

and moonbeams lighting your way.

Boys

Boys You are warriors—born of ancient fire,

carrying the strength of ages past.

Your resolve is unbreakable, your spirits forged
like steel,

rising unbowed against the storms of life.

You are hunters—sharp and relentless,

tracking truth through tangled wilds,

finding clarity in chaos.

You move with precision,

guided by instinct and wisdom,

seeking only what is worthy.

You are kings—

rulers of kindness and grace,

your power measured not in dominion,

but in the light you leave behind.

May your choices stay rooted,

your strength tempered by humility,

and your path carved with purpose.

And know this:

you are not only my sons.

You are my legacy, my triumph,

my eternal roar into the void.

Chosen

Family isn't etched in blood;

it's carved into the unseen places—

the steady hands that catch you

when the world is falling.

It's the warmth of an embrace,

sunlight melting frost,

the voice that calls your name

like a lighthouse through the storm.

Family comes from unexpected places:

a stranger's outstretched hand,

a friend's unshakable loyalty,

the ones who rise from the edges

when those bound by blood turn away.

Blood ties can break,

splintering like brittle glass.

But these bonds are forged in fire—

in deliberate acts of love,

in roots planted beside yours,

steadying you

when the ground shifts beneath your feet.

Family isn't where you began.

It's where you are seen in full,

where broken pieces are gathered gently,

where you can unravel

without fear of being abandoned.

Undeserving

It's strange, isn't it?

The ones who overfill the cup,

watch it spill across the table,

then glare at the puddle

as if it owes them an apology.

They drop puzzle pieces

just to see how far they'll scatter,

then wait for someone else

to kneel and gather them back—

never once bending their own hands.

And still, they stand tall

in the chaos they've created,

arms outstretched,

waiting for grace to fall

like rain they believe was promised.

While those who tread lightly,

who wipe their own spills,

who pick up what was lost—

they ask for nothing,

expect nothing,

yet they are the ones

who should have been given it all.

Heirs

I paint my face in careful strokes,

hiding the parts of me

they could never love.

I soften my voice to be heard—

but raise it, and suddenly I'm too much.

They say, Be yourself,

so long as it's only

the version they want to see.

Perspective

I used to hate my hands—

the rough edges, the scars that told too much,

the way they clenched

when I thought no one was watching.

Now I see their strength:

how they've carried every weight,

how they've held on when I wanted to let go,

how they've built a life

from pieces I thought too broken to keep.

My thighs, once scorned, mocked by mirrors

and whispers in my head, now feel powerful—

pillars of strength that carried me through

storms, roots that dug deep

when the ground crumbled beneath me. They are

no longer shameful;

they are monuments

to everything I've survived.

The scars I wear, once wounds I hid from the
world, now gleam like badges. Uneven edges
speak louder than words: I am here.

I endured. What I once begged to erase is now
sacred.

etched proof of battles fought,

and the courage to keep breathing.

Even the stretch of my stomach,

soft and lined like weathered silk, tells its story—

not of flaws, but of life created,

of a body that held more than I believed it could.

The shadows beneath my eyes are no longer
exhaustion;

they are wisdom,

earned in the quiet hours

186

when I stitched myself back together.

Every piece of me I once despised

is now a masterpiece of survival.

Not flawless,

but radiant in its truth.

I see the beauty now—

in the curves,

in the scars,

in the imperfect lines that trace the map of a life

lived fully.

I have become the woman I never thought I could

be.

Not just whole, but luminous—

a creation of love

for every part of myself

I once couldn't bear to see.

Randomness

I trip over air,

stumble on shadows, and somehow

even a flat surface conspires against me.

My ankles are traitors, my hands disasters—

coffee spills, plates tumble,

doors close just a second too soon.

I've bumped into walls that weren't even in my

way,

knocked over chairs

with the elegance of a wrecking ball,

and let's not even talk about the time the stairs

won.

They call me clumsy,

but I call it flair—

a unique choreography of chaos

that keeps life interesting.

Who needs grace

when you've got the confidence

to fall like it's intentional?

Stargazing

I look up, and the cosmos stretches infinite, each

star a luminous thread in a tapestry of eternity.

How can something so incomprehensible

fit within my gaze,

my fleeting thoughts,

this fragile vessel of flesh and time? The

mountains ascend like ancient psalms,

their jagged peaks whispering reverence.

The oceans thunder with primordial hymns,

each wave a testament

to the vastness of creation.

Even the trees—their branches etching the sky—

and the delicate geometry of a single leaf

speak of an artistry too perfect to be happenstance.

The minutiae astound me:

the spiral of a seashell,

the synchronized hum of a bee, sunlight splintering

through storm clouds, painting the world in

celestial gold. Every detail feels deliberate,

a fragment of infinity hidden in the everyday.

This universe is no accident.

It is poetry set in motion,

a symphony of light and life—

each note precise,

each moment too beautiful

to be anything less

than the work of God's exquisite hand.

Wildlings

They believe they can contain us,

as if fire could be tempered

or hurricanes coaxed into calm.

Their words—restrictions disguised as reason—

amuse me,

for no leash can bind the untamable,

no hand can clasp the feral grace

of a woman unyielding as the wind.

Gaslight

You think your lies are clever,

layers of silk veiling the truth,

each word spun like a spider's thread—

delicate enough to deceive.

But I see the cracks,

the fraying edges of your facade,

the flicker of guilt behind your smile.

I've stood in rooms thick with smoke,

watched illusions curl like paper in flame.

Your tricks are clumsy,

your shadows too shallow to hide in.

Gaslight all you want;

I see the match,

its sulfur lingering in the air

long after your words fade.

Batched

You called me chosen,

but your love burned cold—

a gift wrapped in lies.

You didn't hold me;

you hollowed me,

leaving cracks where hope once lived.

Trust is a trick now,

every hand a question,

every word a blade.

You left,

but the echo stayed,

a constant whisper:

Love is not safe.

Dawn

I have carried a life of shadows,

each moment steeped in sacrifice,

each breath a hymn to endurance.

Pain has etched itself

into the architecture of my soul,

and love—

love has always been a distant shore,

seen but never touched.

Yet even in this desolation,

I feel the fragile promise of tomorrow,

its light trembling on the edge of my horizon.

Hope, tenuous and defiant,

threads itself through the cracks of my ruin,

whispering truths I am desperate to believe:

The darkness will break,

and I will rise with the sun.

Echoes

A single note, and I am unmoored,

time collapsing beneath the weight of familiar

chords.

Each melody is a thread,

pulling me through the fabric of forgotten

moments,

the air thick with memory

I can suddenly breathe again.

The harmonies swell, opening doors

to rooms I thought sealed—

laughter suspended in the air,

tears etched into the silence,

fragments of a life

I didn't know I still carried.

Music doesn't just play;

it reverberates, weaving the past into the present,

reminding me that time is never truly linear,

and some moments are meant to be lived twice.

Traveler

He stares at the stars,

a restless Aries flame,

burning with questions too big for this earth.

The planets shimmer like whispers,

distant worlds spinning secrets,

waiting for his hands to reach

what no one else has touched.

He doesn't see limits—only doors,

the vast sky a map etched with wonder.

The universe isn't far;

it's his,

and he was born to claim it.

The Willow

I grew up like a lone tree

in a field of neatly planted rows,

my branches twisting freely, reaching for a sky

they couldn't measure.

Their words fell like axes,

their stares colder than shadows,

and they tried—oh, how they tried—

to shape me into a symmetry

I was never meant to fit.

Different felt like exile—

isolated, aching,

the weight of standing apart

in a world that praised sameness.

But my roots found the depths,

where their rigid lines couldn't follow.

Now I rise unyielding,

a silhouette against their monotony,

a quiet strength

they will never understand.

Individually

I am the only one of me,

crafted from storms no one else has weathered,

a mosaic of cracks and resilience

that no hands but mine could shape.

I've walked paths littered with shadows,

faced nights that swallowed light whole,

and I've come out the other side—

not unscathed, but unshakable.

They said I wouldn't make it,

but here I stand,

a phoenix rising from ash they thought final,

each scar a thread in the tapestry

of who I've become.

I am not just alive—

I am astonishing,

a testament to the impossible,

proof that mountains can move

when the heart refuses to yield.

If I can rise, so can you.

Whatever haunts your story,

whatever tried to shatter you,

remember:

even the darkest skies

can't extinguish the brilliance

of a star that refuses to burn out.

Acknowledgment

To The Creator,

For the trials that broke me open and the storms
that carved me into who I am.

For every moment of suffering that carried within
it the seeds of growth, for the endurance that built
my strength, and for the quiet grace that held me
together when I felt I would fall apart.

You took my pain and gave it purpose, turned my
wounds into words, and transformed my heartache
into something that could touch others.

Through everything, You walked beside me.
Through the darkest nights, You lit my way.

Thank You for showing me that even in
brokenness, there is beauty—and through creation,
there is healing. Thank You for shaping this
collection into something I never imagined it could
be.

To my big brother, Jason,

Thank You for always loving me, even when I was an absolute pain, and for setting the bar so high with your strength, loyalty, and love for family. You were the person I always looked up to (even when I pretended I didn't), and the one who helped shape the kind of mother I grew up to be.

I hope this book makes you proud because I'm pretty sure making my big brother proud has always been one of my secret goals. Thank you for being such an incredible example through the years.

With Love, Your still slightly bratty but endlessly grateful little sister

To Elaine, Thank you for opening the doors to worlds I had never imagined and for placing books in my hands that lit my curiosity and shaped my dreams.

You shared stories that became part of me, teaching me to see life through new perspectives and discover the magic in words. The books you introduced to me as a child were more than stories—they were seeds, growing into a love of literature that continues to guide my path. Your gift lives on in every word I write and every story I share.

To the calm to my wild, the steady to my storm, the one who holds me together when I feel like falling apart: without your persistence, your unwavering belief in me, and the quiet strength you offer every day, this would never have been possible.

You've always seen the best in me, even when I was too lost or afraid to see it myself. Your love, your faith, and your refusal to let me give up have been the foundation of everything I've accomplished.

You are my anchor when the world feels unsteady, my courage when doubts creep in, and the reason I believe in the beauty of dreaming in this world.

And to you, my readers,

who now hold this book in your hands: know that you are the soul of this creation.

This is for you—the beautifully broken, the endlessly resilient, the ones who rise despite it all. Thank you for letting my words find a home in your heart and for being a part of this journey with me.

Cinder & Ivy

www.ingramcontent.com/pod-product-compliance
Lightning Source LLC
Chambersburg PA
CBHW030221140626
46545CB00011B/391